FEATHERED FARM ANIMALS

GEESE

by Elizabeth Andrews

Cody Koala

An Imprint of Pop!
popbooksonline.com

Hello! My name is Cody Koala

This book is filled with videos, puzzles, games, and more! Scan the QR codes* while you read, or visit the website below to make this book pop.

popbooksonline.com/goose

*Scanning QR codes requires a web-enabled smart device with a QR code reader app and a camera.

abdobooks.com

Published by Pop!, a division of ABDO, PO Box 398166, Minneapolis, Minnesota 55439.

Printed in the United States of America, North Mankato, Minnesota.

082025
012026

Cover Photo: Shutterstock Images
Interior Photos: Shutterstock Images; Getty Images
Editors: Tyler Gieseke and Grace Hansen
Series Designer: Julia Line

Library of Congress Control Number: 2025940514

Publisher's Cataloging-in-Publication Data
Names: Andrews, Elizabeth, author.
Title: Geese / by Elizabeth Andrews
Description: Minneapolis, Minnesota : Pop!, 2026 | Series: Feathered farm animals | Includes online resources and index
Identifiers: ISBN 9781098248550 (lib. bdg.) | ISBN 9781098249076 (ebook)
Subjects: LCSH: Geese--Juvenile literature. | Poultry--Juvenile literature. | Fowls--Juvenile literature. | Farm animals--Juvenile literature. | Animal husbandry--Juvenile literature.
Classification: DDC 636.598--dc23

Table of Contents

Chapter 1

Meet the Goose!

Geese are birds. They live in groups called flocks or gaggles. Male geese are called ganders. Females are just called geese. They are raised for their meat, eggs, and feathers.

Geese honk, cackle, and hiss.

Geese are covered in feathers. Farmers raise ten **breeds** of geese. Common farm geese are the cotton

patch and American buff. They are usually gray or white with orange beaks and feet.

Geese grow to be about 2.5 to 2.8 feet (0.8–0.9 m) long. They weigh 8 to 12 pounds (3.6–5.4 kg). Their feathers are covered in a special oil that makes them unaffected by water. Their feet are **webbed**.

Goose feathers are used to make warm clothes and bedding.

beak

wing

tail

paunch

webbed foot

Female geese start laying eggs at nine months old. They can lay 30 to 50 eggs a year. Their eggs are three times bigger than chicken eggs.

Chapter 2

Life on the Farm

Farm geese spend much of their day looking for food. They become friendly with other animals on their farm and the humans who look after them.

Learn more here!

Geese are known for being **aggressive** birds. Sometimes they are kept on farms as protectors. The geese watch for **intruders** and honk loudly at anything strange.

Geese learn which animals are meant to be on the farm and which are not. They won't honk at farm cats or dogs once they get to know them.

Geese like to be outside during the day. They don't need to be in water, but they

enjoy it. They need a safe and warm place, such as a **coop** or barn, to sleep.

Chapter 3

What Do They Eat?

Geese usually eat greens. They tear at grasses with the teeth in their beaks. Geese are often kept on farms to eat weeds in gardens. They won't eat the main plants. Geese also need fresh water.

Geese will eat worms, snails, and insects, but they like grasses better.

Chapter 4

Fluffy Goslings

Baby geese are called goslings. They **hatch** from eggs. They are covered in soft feathers called down. Geese can swim right away. They start finding their own food at five to six weeks old.

Complete an activity here!

Making Connections

Text-to-Self

What is one new thing that you learned about geese from this book?

Text-to-Text

Have you read any other books about farm animals? How are those animals similar to or different from geese?

Text-to-World

Goose isn't often eaten in the US. With the help of an adult, look up where people eat goose. What kinds of dishes do they make with goose meat?

Glossary

aggressive – pushy and willing to fight.

breed – a specific type of an animal that is raised by humans.

coop – a small enclosed space to house farm birds.

hatch – to break out of an egg.

intruder – someone who enters a place where they aren't supposed to be.

webbed – having thin skin connecting the toes.

Index

Online Resources

popbooksonline.com

Thanks for reading this Cody Koala book!

This book is filled with videos, puzzles, games, and more! Scan the QR codes* while you read, or visit the website below to make this book pop.

*Scanning QR codes requires a web-enabled smart device with a QR code reader app and a camera.